Essential Tips for
Coaching Youth Sports

By **Dan Cowan**

Essential Tips for Coaching Youth Sports

Author: Dan Cowan

Published by Austin Brothers Publishing

Fort Worth, Texas

www.austinbrotherspublishing.com

ISBN: 978-0-9845366-5-8

This and other books published by
Austin Brothers Publishing
can be purchased at -
www.austinbrotherspublishing.com

Printed in the United States of America
2015 -- First Edition

ABP
Austin Brothers Publishing
www.austinbrotherspublishing.com

Dedication

Thank you to everyone who has supported or influenced me along the way. My hope is that this book can be a useful tool for coaches. The influence of many has helped and motivated me to get this published to impact youth sports around the country. People I would like to thank include teammates, family, coaches, and colleagues. Thank you to Lav, Ed, Matt, Bethy, Adam, Mom, Dad, Mr. R., Ralph, Mike B, Will, Steve, Paul, Jeff, Josh, Ricke, Jordan, Red, Murph, Trac, Rodney, Shayla, Sara Winston, Carlos, Sonia, Moorsey, Dr. Bart, and Dr. Lutz.

My sister Bethy, you have been valuable taking the vision and crafting it to make it visible.

My brother Matt, the hours and effort you have put forth have been crucial. Bouncing off ideas, making sure the message resonates, keeping me organized, on task, and sane. We keep grinding. Thank you!

My beautiful family Isaac, Layne, and Lauren; your love has been unfathomably patient and supportive. God has blessed me with an amazing family and support network. I hope these words and experiences speak to you as well!

I want to thank my Lord and Savior for putting this passion and goal in my heart; giving me the strength to walk down a path that wasn't highly visible. I pray the wisdom He provided comes through in this book, and can resonate with all who take a moment to read it.

/

The Coaching Tips

Introduction

Coaching is an amazing opportunity to influence the lives and development of young people across the country, and especially in your own community. This book was designed to assist you with their development as well as your development as a coach and mentor. Throughout this book we have provided tips and details that will assist you in this journey. The goal of youth sports should be to introduce young individuals to a sport as well as learn life lessons.

Those lessons will include team building, overcoming obstacles, and self-worth, along with many more issues that will help shape them as they grow. They come from different backgrounds and circumstances, and as their coach you need to be aware of their situation. In addition to teaching a sport, you have the opportunity to teach life coping skills as well as build healthy relationships.

Many athletes have pointed to sports as their one outlet that saved them from a bad situation. It might not be the sport itself, but a coach or teammate who was willing to listen and encourage them in their life. Something as simple as listening, or just taking an interest in that individual was enough to keep them out of prison, gangs, depression, and possibly suicide. A coach has the amazing opportunity to positively impact more lives in one season than most people will in their entire life. It is mind blowing to think about it as most people that coach do it because they love it. They aren't looking for someone to keep score on the number of lives they impact. There is genuine concern for the youth athletes.

This book will challenge your approach, and even shed light on why athletes think and act the way they do. Challenge you in a way that will help you understand your behavior and approach, and serve to sharpen your skills. The kids understanding and approach will surprise you, and that can be both bad and good. Some will showcase a deeper understanding of the game and situation than you realized, and there will be others just repeating what you said, but with no understanding of why it is correct.

People tend to get wrapped up in the game and forget about the life and outside environmental factors that are ever present, but might not be highly visible. Think about when there is an injury during a game, everyone gets quiet and the focus switches to a hope that the young athlete is alright since their health and welfare is bigger than the game. This is what we want to keep present in our mind—that the overall health and welfare of these kids are bigger than any game, and the one that needs to keep it on the minds of everyone else is you, their COACH!

Enjoy the tips and feel free to share this with friends and other coaches. We would love your feedback and stories for our next book. We hope to run into you on a field, court, mat, pool, or somewhere across the country with this book rolled up and worn in your coach's bag.

The Coaching Tips

Keep the Playing Area Safe

Coaches should always check the field of play before every game. Check for safety issues, obstructions, or any other issues that might affect the play of your team. This can be done with a quick walk through by yourself or an assistant coach. This is simple, but it is one of the most over-looked steps and procedures in coaching. Coaches assume that the league, city, or organization has done their due diligence with every field or playing surface. When in reality they lean on coaches, officials, and parents to bring up any deficiencies.

For indoor sports, there shouldn't be too much in the way of differences. You should still check the net, floor, markings, and boundaries. In hockey this could be looking at the boards, glass, benches, ice condition, and nets. Make sure the boundaries are understood by your team, or if there is any confusion, clear it up before the game.

For outdoor sports, this can be a little trickier. Baseball and softball fields will naturally be different with the grass, dirt, or turf. Check the mound for stability and a solid landing point for your pitcher. Ensure proper distance to home plate, and the bases are correct due to various age groups utilizing the same fields. Check the outfield for any holes in the ground and surrounding fences. This is the same for football and soccer. Make sure there are not any holes created by critters that could severely hurt your players. Markings and boundaries will also vary depending on how the field is utilized. There could be multiple sports that have alternate boundaries and marking that can cause confusion.

Spending a few moments before each game might not give you a competitive advantage, but it can save you from a catastrophe.

Learn How to Hear What Parents are Saying

Coaches, listen to the parents on your team. You don't have to agree with them or get into an argument, just hear them out. You can respond with: "I'll take that into consideration," "Thanks for your input," or "I appreciate you bringing this to my attention." Listening to what they have to say will help disarm any tension that is building off the field.

Parents are looking for an outlet for their concern. If they are able to approach you they can let you know what is bothering them. Most likely they will want to talk about positions and playing time, but there is a chance it could be some information that will help you and your team.

It will also help increase your creditability and build allies with the parents. This is not to say the parents are against you as a coach, but it will help to disarm any conversations that happen in the stands while you are focused on the game. It is common in the stands of sporting events to second guess the coach. You can help combat this issue if you have built a solid relationship with the parents. If anyone does start the second guessing, parents will step up to back you up, and support your decisions.

This will help to build loyalty with the parents, and when the kids look to their parents to see if you know what you are talking about, the parents will back you up again. Now you are building team cohesion. Your message and instruction will get through to your team and have a higher tendency to stick.

There is a time and place for these conversations to happen. Don't let them happen during the game or in the middle of instruction or practice.

Know Your Team and Why They are There

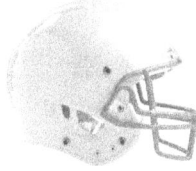

Coaches need to take extra time to learn why your players are on your team. Are they there to learn the sport, interact with other kids their age, are their parents making them play, etc. There are many reasons kids join a sports league. Spend a few extra moments to learn about them and their reasons.

Being a coach is much more than teaching a game. It is about being a positive role model for the kids, and helping them see the obstacles in life and overcome them. Kids today are under a large amount of pressure from tests, family life, social media, peer pressure, and just regular development. Everything and everyone are fighting for their attention; everything they do is quantified and measured. Parents are frequently pushing them to be the star player on the team, not just one of the players.

Sometimes kids just want a break from all of the madness and pressure and to just play with their friends. They might be looking for an adult who can be a neutral party to their crazy family situation. Their home environment might have their parents fighting all of time, never at home because of work or other reasons, blended families, recent death or disease diagnosis. The point is that sometimes a kid just wants a brief moment to unload their stress and baggage they are carrying. A score or game takes the backseat to enjoying a moment of life before picking up the stress and baggage and heading back to their situation.

Communicate at the Appropriate Level

Proper communication is key for development. Six-year-olds don't communicate the same way as ten-year-olds. Their understanding levels will differ even at the same age. Make sure to ask for feedback. It is important to know what they think you want them to do.

A common mistake is to yell in order to tell the kids what to do. The coach thinks it is clear instruction, but the kid isn't processing the information for one reason or another. Feedback is a good way to understand how the child processes information, retains information, and can reproduce the instruction.

Attention span for a child today is 8.5 seconds! (See page 21) It is a small window for a coach to provide instruction and keep the young athlete on task. Feedback will help a coach understand how much of the information got through. It could be that demonstration is the best way over pure instruction, or a mix is the most effective way. As a coach, always evolve and be alert to how your team hears and interprets your information.

Prepare for Emergencies

It is a good idea to designate one of your parents to be in charge of off the field safety issues. Have someone ready to react in case a situation arises. This could be as simple as ready to call 9-1-1, or make sure there is plenty of water during the hot summer months. Not only is it best practices to help reaction time for safety issues, but also provides an opportunity to have parents involved with the team, instead of just being a spectator.

A real life situation that happened during a game was when one of the player's siblings was playing in the parking lot. The parents were focused on the game. The sibling was struck by a car in the parking lot. Thankfully it wasn't a serious injury and the child was fine. A parent will tend to panic due to the high stress of the situation, and there is a need to have someone with a clear head and action plan ready to go. Having someone assigned to make the call for help gives a clear communication path and plan of action. It will cut down on any unnecessary delay for help.

Having parents involved in the team also helps with a positive interaction and experience with the coach and team. They will have a sense of ownership and involvement with the team. This will also take a piece of the workload from you so you can focus on your team and the game.

Protecting Your Communication with Parents

With email communication to your team, always Blind Carbon Copy (BCC) your distribution list. What this means is to put the recipients email address in the "BCC" line rather than the "To" line. This will create a clean communication chain, knowing only important information will come from the team. Keeping it clean will deter anyone from responding to everyone, and turning it into a gossip thread.

Information from the coach is important, as it might include change information about time, location, uniform, and other vital information for the team. Things change on a regular basis due to various reasons, and having a clear communication chain will reduce any confusion for the individuals on the team. It will keep everyone on the same page and prepared.

There are times when everyone can respond with their input, and it ends up being a 30+ email message chain, and the vital pieces of information get lost. Keep it clean and clear from one source.

Real world example: The league organizers had a disagreement with a coach, and through the distribution list publicly accused the others of stealing money from the league since it wasn't kept private. This destroyed the credibility of the league and the coach. Parents and players left looking for another league. It doesn't matter if the accusations were true or not, they did the damage. A simple practice of not releasing the email information could have prevented a big mess and blown season for the kids.

Planning is as Important as Practice

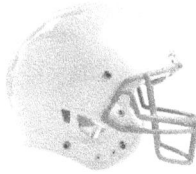

Coaches you should set aside 30 minutes prior to each practice and game for planning. This should include drills, groups, rotations, having the right equipment for drills, positions, substitutions, hydration station, and a completed emergency contact roster. We understand you already spend a lot of your free time volunteering, but this additional planning time will help the season run more smoothly as well as increase the learning opportunity for the kids on your team.

This extra planning will allow you to evaluate your team on a consistent basis and adjust practice accordingly. It will help you build on the fundamentals and skills you have begun to teach. Kids will pick up skills and drills differently so you will be able to pair them up in the best groups.

One of the biggest flaws for practice is the coach who just shows up and wings it. There is no direction or plan to fall back on. Yes, it is easy to go with the same old drills. There is value in repetition, but it isn't maximizing learning and development.

Hydration — an Important Safety Tip

Dehydration is one of the most common injury or health issues in sports. As a coach, you have no information regarding how hydrated a player is prior to practice or a game. It is ideal to ensure and encourage them to drink plenty of water or healthy fluids prior, during, and after practice or competition.

Coaches shouldn't withhold water breaks as punishment or discipline. There are many other ways to get your point across, and creative ways to reach your team without endangering the health of the kids. No coach wants to see kids use water breaks to get out of practice, or take an easy way out, but it shouldn't be a punishment tool. Schedule water break times during practice, and stick to those times.

This is one of those common sense concepts that needs to be repeated frequently. There is a tendency to fall back to the hard core mentality and hammer the point home by pushing kids to their limit. There are ways to do that without withholding water. Heat stroke and heat exhaustion have serious repercussions throughout their life.

Sidenote; be aware of the temperature on the field, turf, court, room, etc. where you practice. Don't just make decisions from the weather forecast. Practice facilities, fields, and turf tend to hold heat, and can create an environment in excess of 20 degrees higher than the forecast.

During a weekend baseball tournament the temperature was in excess of 99 degrees. One of the players, in between games, was given money by his parent for drinks and snacks, and he left the tournament area. This player used the money to buy soda and candy in between games. As the second game got underway, this player complained of being dizzy and sick. He was sat down in the dugout, and his symptoms continued to get worse. Medical personnel were slow to arrive, but other parents helped to provide aid on the instruction of the coach. The player was removed from the game and treated for heat exhaustion and severe dehydration. The parent of this player blamed the coach for not looking out for the health of the player.

As a coach you don't always have all of the information on the hydration level of your athletes. Dehydration and heat exhaustion can come on quickly, and if proper care isn't near by the severity can escalate quickly. Encourage hydration and possible over hydration in light of environmental factors. Don't do anything that promotes dehydration, such as withholding water breaks. Work with parents on their hydration methods of their kids prior, during, and after practices or competitions.

Coaching Kids with a Short Attention Span

One of the more common complaints we hear is that "Kids just don't listen or pay attention!" A coach is trying to run instruction, and the kids are goofing off and horse playing. The coach gets frustrated and yells at them. The kids turn their eyes to the coach only to turn away seconds later and go back to goofing off. Sound familiar? It happens to all of us. So what can be done other than complain that "Kids these days, just don't listen!"

Are kids these days different? The answer is a resounding yes. They are being bombarded by information constantly, with multiple stimuli fighting for their attention. They have greater access to information than any previous generation. Statistics from National Center for Biotechnology Information and the U.S. National Library of Medicine shows that the average attention span is 8.25 seconds; down from 12 minutes 25 years ago. Let that sink in, 8.25 seconds! Kids today are asked to process more information in a shorter amount of time. That is the tradeoff—less focus in order to process more information faster.

Companies are spending billions of dollars, $17 billion annually, on marketing and studies so they can reach kids faster.[1]

The average television commercial has dropped from 30 seconds to 15 seconds.[2] No wonder ADHD diagnoses are on the rise. The CDC is reporting that about 11% of kids have ADHD, up from 9% a few years ago.[3] The average cost to treat ADHD is approximately $15K a year per child. Parents often look for alternate ways to keep their child stimulated and engaged other than drugs and medicine. One of the most popular ways to do this is through sports and athletics. Sports provides an outlet for their child to be active and engaged with other kids. They learn lessons such as hard work, determination, focus, overcoming obstacles, teamwork, and building a great sense of self-esteem. Sports provides a more natural and healthy treatment plan through exercise and active lifestyle.

Sports and athletics seem like a perfect fit to help kids with short attention spans or attention issues. The methods used should be relevant to the learning style of kids and young athletes today. Don't be a coach still trying to use the

---

1   James McNeil quoted in Horovitz, B. 2006, November 22, *Six Strategies Marketers use to Make Kids Want Things Bad,* USA Today, p. 1B. Retrieved March 2, 2008, from http://www.usatoday.com/money/advertising/2006-11-21-toy-strategies-usat...

2   http://betterbusiness.torkusa.com/marketing-to-the-shrinking-attention-span-of-the-modern-consumer/.

3   http://www.cdc.gov/ncbddd/adhd/data.html.

drills and methods learned when you were young. Methods and drills that held the coach's attention when they were young are not necessarily stimulating enough for kids today.

So, how should kids, who have been conditioned by society to have less focus and process information faster, be coached? First, identify the area that should be fixed or taught. It is crucial to understand the desired outcome. Design a drill focused specifically on that area or movement.

Let's use the example of a baseball team that struggles with throws to a nearby base. During games, the players keep trying to do an overhand throw that leads to the receiving player dropping the ball, or not completing the catch. The area that should change is to make the throw an underhand toss. This will keep the ball in a catchable area and allows the throwing player more control in getting the ball to the right location.

Break into small groups, roughly 3-4 kids. Keeping interaction confined to a small group keeps them on task. You can do the same drill with the other groups in order to keep as many kids actively engaged as possible. Let's continue to use our example. Break into groups of three. Get into a triangle and pass the ball underhand to each of the other players. Have them change direction to simulate throwing to other bags. This is a quick drill and will go fast. This keeps everyone engaged, and they will have to pay attention in order to complete it properly.

You can then take that movement or drill and add it into a larger drill. Again, staying with our example, use one kid to act as the player fielding the ball. They will turn and underhand toss it to another kid who will act like they are on the base. They can touch or tag an imaginary runner. The third kid can throw grounders to the first keeping the triangle going. Again, everyone is involved and can rotate through the drill.

Finally, all of it can be added into a game situation. Expand and add extra team members. Continuing to add onto the drill and situation will keep things new and fresh. The kids should still be paying attention and involved. Expanding to game situations, the team can still be split, but in larger groups. The groups can be put into competition with each other. For our example, make one group the fielders and the other group the base runners. Switch groups after three outs, and recap after each team has had the opportunity to execute the skill. Remind the team what they should have learned and the correct way to execute the skill.

In this case, we have taken one instance and focused on a small issue and built it out to a game situation. All of the kids will stay involved and on task. We kept teaching to small groups, instructions were simple and brief. They will be able to process this information and complete the correct mechanical movement.

Another issue that can arise and cause frustration is information overload. Once overload happens additional conversation can become white noise and will cause players to ignore instructions, and when they start to ignore a coach, the coach needs to get them back on task.

It is a difficult thing especially if the player is at a spot where they can't handle any more information. The coach needs to come up with a divider. A divider can be a useful mechanism to help continue with learning. A divider will create space in the mind of an athlete that lets them section off learning. A good example of this is a phone number. Numbers are spaced and divided by a dash, so individuals can remember blocks of numbers. The dash acts as a divider or mechanism used to maintain larger amounts of information.

A coach can use something like running a quick sprint as a divider. This is better than using a water break as a divider. A water break allows the players to socialize and disengage. To be clear, we are not suggesting ignoring water breaks. Rather do a drill, sprint, do another drill, sprint, do another drill, give a water break, sprint, and do another drill. In this example a sprint is used as a divider between drills. At the end of each sprint the players know another drill is coming and they will be ready to focus or the next instruction.

Another reason for not paying attention or being distracted is a player thinking about a bad play, or some other issue that is occupying their mind. The coach needs to have a reset button for the players. This should be something physical that the players can touch and use to reset and re-focus their mind. It can be a piece of equipment, picture, plaque, or some other item that will signal to the mind and body to let go and reset the mind to the next portion of the game.

One of the most popular stories over a reset button was the Cal State Fullerton baseball team using a mini toilet as their reset button. If they made a bad play, or had a bad at bat, the players would come in and flush the mini toilet. This would allow for the players to forget about the bad play and refocus on the next job or task. They won the college baseball national championship that season.

Having players that aren't focused or paying attention is a product of the current society. Just because kids today have reduced attention spans, it doesn't mean they are unable to learn. It means that teaching has to be adjusted appropriately. They are growing up daily with so many things fighting for their attention. They are conditioned to process information quickly, and then look for the next item that stimulates their mind.

Coaches need to understand and make the appropriate changes to adapt to a different learning style of kids today. Practices should be focused on keeping the team involved at all times, with the drills broken up by a divider in order to reset and keep their focus.

This may seem to be a daunting task to change methods and approaches that have been used for years, but with a little planning, it can be achieved by any coach.

Know Your Team — Supervision

Coaches need to pay extra attention to the kids whose parents treat sports like a babysitting service. Make sure you know who will be the point of contact in case of an injury, and how long will it take for their parent/guardian to get there? If the parent(s) are uninterested in the child's sports, do you think they spend extra time outside to be highly involved in that child's interest? This isn't the case in every situation, but it is something to take into consideration.

Expectations should be set with the parents at the beginning of the season that practice is not a babysitting service, or time to get away for happy hour. Accidents and injuries happen in practice more frequently than in games. Someone needs to be available just in case an injury or situation occurs that will require parental action. It will also help with building team cohesion around your teaching methods with the parents. They will see how the kids are practicing and the fundamental skills you are teaching.

These will be the kids who are at a higher risk for negative behavior as they continue to develop, so they will need a positive mentor in their life. Take a few minutes throughout the season to talk to them about things they like or don't like. Something as simple as a short conversation can have a lifelong impression.

I recently had a conversation with an individual who had no positive parental involvement in his life. He was in jail because of a bad situation with his aunt who had become his primary care giver. He was on the verge of suicide, and contemplated it many times. His desperation turned to hope through prayer, and was introduced to a coach who helped young athletes in a bad neighborhood. This coach would train young athletes to keep them out of bad situations, and their only payment was a bible verse.

This one interaction transformed this individual, and he went on to finish school despite being homeless. He continued to practice what he learned from his coach. He went on to become a pro football player and won a Super Bowl. He is still in touch with this coach, and he continues to help kids in the same manner.

Know Your Team — Goal Setting

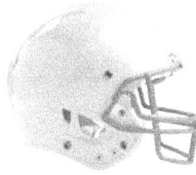

Make sure to set clear goals with the athlete and relay those goals to the parents. Kids have expectations put on them by their parents, knowingly or unknowingly. The pressure at home may be more than what is expected from the team, at any age. This can simply be done by telling the athlete, in the presence of the parent(s), "our focus this season is X, we will help you get there by Y." This will take the pressure off the athlete and let them know how to set their focus and expectations. Granted there can be more to this process, but this is a simple first step.

Goal setting can be tricky but there should be a long term goal with short term goals as steps in between. It is a process, and everyone involved should understand that it is a process. Overbearing parents want their kids to be perfect, and tend to remind them when they make a mistake. Kids are going to make mistakes, and they have to understand that mistakes are ok and part of the learning process. Parents need to know that as well.

Goals should be established together with the athlete with their input. Goals should stretch the athlete, but should also be attainable. Goals that are easily attainable don't really help the athlete. Highly attainable goals can be used as early short term goals so they feel like they are making progress and will want to knock out the next milestone.

Give Attention to Detail

Coaches with different levels of experience can benefit from a coaching class, even if the class is viewed as redundant. Experience throughout the season might bring on a different view or take on how to handle it the next time around.

The key is continued focus on the small issues that can have large, long-lasting ramifications. New situations provide new perspectives on how to handle situations. Taking continuing education courses or researching certain subjects should be second nature for coaches to help them handle future situations.

As coaches, we ask our athletes to continue to improve then why shouldn't we as coaches be doing the same? Even if the material doesn't provide any new direct insight, it is good to have simply as a reminder.

As a leader, continue to lead from the front, and search for new ways to improve or new ways to look at situations that can be passed along to your athletes.

Sports Should Include Fun

Not once in my adult life has anyone been concerned about how much any of my youth teams won or lost. Having a good time with the others on the team is what truly mattered. That particular sport might not be what everyone wants to do when they get older.

As adults, we don't care or think twice about other adults' childhood teams, or even their records. We see them as people, separate from their youth accomplishments or lack of accomplishments. This isn't the case for a lot of people these days, and has changed the way they view their kids in sports. They want their kids to win now at all costs, and continue to win without building a solid foundation.

The biggest factor for success in sports, or even a career in sports, is if a player loves the sport. This is measured through intrinsic vs. extrinsic motivation. People who are intrinsically motivated are driven by internal pleasure and motives, they have higher performance than the individuals motivated by external rewards. Let the kids fall in love with it in their own time, and they will be more successful down the road. This is true even if they don't stick with sports, they will form bonds and lifelong memories, and life skills.

Here is a task for you: Find an old team picture. As you look at the faces what comes to mind first? Is it the bond you had with them? The team record?

Always Look For Ways to Improve

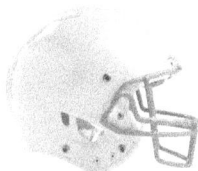

Just because something is *the way we have always done it*, doesn't mean it is the best way to keep doing it. People have a tendency to get in ruts and stop looking for better ways to teach or approach issues.

The games that we teach and the kids we coach continue to change. Your methods of teaching should also evolve. First think about the kids and how this generation is different from the kids 20 years ago. Attention span has dropped from 12 minutes down to 8.5 seconds. The same ways to coach an athlete won't be as effective. Next think about football, going from a heavy run and defense mentality to spread offense and video game scores. These are just a couple of many examples of how kids and the games are changing.

Change is inevitable, and the coaches who are willing to accept that and adapt with the game and kids will be more successful in the long run.

Don't Let Good Sportsmanship Slip Away

Bad behavior from parents or athletes should not be tolerated or accepted as commonplace in youth sports. Turning a blind eye or deaf ear is a passive way to accept this behavior. As a coach, people will watch your behavior to see what is tolerable.

In youth sports, the fans are viewed as an extension of the team. A coach needs to set expectations with the parents and fans at the beginning of the season. It is much easier to deal with this issue before the season than during the season. It starts small, but grows out of hand rapidly. This usually starts with spectators making fun of a kid on the other team. It might not be loud, and just among a couple of people. Then it starts to turn into yelling so the kids can hear it. Once it gets to that point, most people will look to the coach to see your reaction. The majority of people know that it is wrong, but usually take the silent route instead of a confrontation.

The confrontation should not escalate to a physical altercation. This is why, as a team, you should have rules and procedures in place. The first time is a warning, and the second time is removal from the event. If a spectator is removed, inform the league with as much detail as possible. The spectator should have to take a behavioral course or some type of code of conduct training before returning.

Distribute the rules and procedures at the beginning of the season. Don't be caught in a situation that can be avoided with the proper steps. The kids and parents will be taking their cues from you on what is acceptable.

Learn to Communicate What You Know

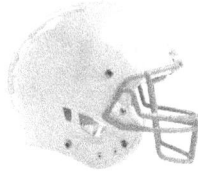

Having a great deal of knowledge doesn't mean much if you can't properly relate and explain it to your team and athletes. One of the biggest misconceptions in youth sports is that experience is the same as coaching ability. This is proven to be wrong time and time again at every level of play. Michael Jordan was the greatest basketball player and a savvy business executive, but he didn't make a great coach. This is because he couldn't relate to players what it took to be exceptional. This takes nothing away from his playing accomplishments, but it is one example of having experience doesn't mean the same as coaching ability.

Learn to relate and talk with your players. Look them in the eyes, be on their level, ask for feedback, and listen to them. You will build a bond with them and they will be more receptive to your instruction.

Understand What is Important

Since *participation* awards are being given out, there is a big misconception that exists that kids don't know how to win or lose. This isn't true. A kid's self worth isn't based off winning or losing at a younger age. Adults put their own self worth into their kid winning or losing—did they buy them the right equipment, hire a special trainer, work them out enough, etc. Many are worried if that makes them a good parent or bad parent.

Adults should be more concerned about the quality time they put in with their kids. Teach them about respect, dignity, hard work, ethics, sportsmanship, perseverance, and being a good teammate. Kids understand winning and losing, but most don't put a heavy burden on it because they know they will have more opportunities.

They are playing for more than just winning and losing. They might be playing for their friends, parents, grandparents, to get out of the house, nothing else to do, and other various reasons. Kids who enjoy the sport will stick with it.

Most will have fun while they are young, and then move in a different direction as they grow and mature.

Participation awards won't be satisfying for the kids who want to pursue athletics whole heartedly when they get older. They will develop that drive and urge to push themselves to their limits. The kids that are in sports for their friends will appreciate the recognition, and use the award to look back fondly on the time with a team of friends.

We had a happy go lucky kid who would come to wrestling practice to enjoy the time around friends. He worked just as hard as the other kids in the room during practice, but his goal wasn't to be the best wrestler. At one tournament he received a medal because there were not enough kids in his bracket. He snuck that medal into his class pictures. I used to be opposed to giving medals and awards that weren't earned, but after seeing his behavior and how excited he was with his medal, it changed my perspective.

That medal for him served as a reminder of the fun he was having with his friends and coaches. He put in the work by his commitment in practice and continued to get back on the mat for his next match. The color of the medal or place wasn't what was important, but rather it was what the medal meant to him.

The Kind of Coach Kid's Desire

One of the biggest reasons leagues put up with bad coaches is that they claim they can't replace their knowledge or experience. They will bully other coaches, kids, parents, officials, and board members. They will make outlandish claims such as, "Do you know who I am?" "I'm friends with so and so!" or "That doesn't apply to me!"

To me personally, it raises red flags when a coach doesn't want to continue to change or try to get better. I wouldn't want that individual in my organization or coaching my child, it wouldn't matter how much experience they have or knowledge they claim to have. They are a destructive force, and will make the team and league weaker in the long run.

Are you a coach you would want to play for? Would you be proud if your child coached just like you?

Don't be Satisfied With Your Approach

Coaches must keep an open mind and constantly ask themselves, "Can I be better?" "Can I run practice differently to improve learning?" "Is there anything else I can do, or even stop doing, that would help the team develop?"

Coaching can be filled with a strong ego, but it is truly the coach who can put the ego on the shelf for awhile, and do an honest assessment that will lead to the greatest improvements. There is a fine line between looking for better methods and having self-doubt. Be aware of that danger while communicating to your team.

Be strong and confident in your message, but also remember that other teams can counter your approach. So be prepared to respond to their counter. Knowing how to spot weaknesses and make adjustments will allow you to keep your athletes self-aware and driven for improvements as well. This is a mark of a great coach.

Be Careful with Social Media

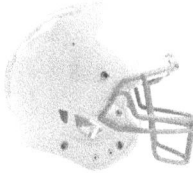

Coaches should avoid interacting with their athletes on social media. If you have a comment, feel free to interact with the parents first. This could be a gray area for athletes as they get to a higher level like high school, college, or professional. A good rule of thumb is just to avoid it.

Social Media is something that is new to this generation, and a new tool for coaches as well. This is a huge area that can do more harm for an athlete than good. As a coach, avoid using this as a communication tool with your athletes. Youth athletes are minors, and interacting with them on a social or private platform can give the wrong impression.

If you need to tag them in a picture or post, do it through their parents. Let the parent make the decision, or share it with them. As a personal safety precaution, just avoid it.

Teach the Proper
Biomechanical Movements

There are techniques being taught that don't encourage proper movement or body position. As a coach, we need to understand the purpose of the movement or drill we are teaching. What should the proper mechanics look like, and how can that be related to the athlete.

For example, the exercise known as *Squashing the Bug* was meant to get a batter to rotate on his back foot specifically on his toes to help with his swing and power. Focusing just on the foot actually hinders the proper biomechanical movement of the swing. The focus should be up on the hips. Getting the hips to rotate will force the leg to rotate. I have used the example of getting the hips to point toward the pitcher, or if you were a cowboy, getting your six-shooter facing the pitcher. Think about what you want to achieve from a movement you are teaching, and ask yourself is it getting the desired result, or is it hindering the result.

There are many resources available to learn and evaluate correct biomechanical movements. I encourage you to reach out to multiple resources and ask their input. Evaluate their responses, and see which ones make sense, and which ones don't, then decide what to incorporate into your practices.

There are also apps for your phone or tablet that will help you record and evaluate proper biomechanical movements. Try to get comfortable with a couple of different applications, or build a relationship with some subject matter experts. All of this will help you teach techniques that are truly helpful for your athletes.

Don't Blame Others for Failure

Parents, and Players: Quit complaining about the ump, ref, and/or judge. Bad calls happen at every level, and everyone knows they happen more frequently at the youth level. Instead, use it as a teaching moment about overcoming obstacles and pushing through setbacks.

Don't leave it in the hands of the ref, judge, or ump. There are many other times to take care of business and execute.

If a player hears everyone blaming someone else, they have an excuse not to take responsibility, and then no one improves. Excuses make nobody better, and are a weak attempt to shift blame.

If the public openness of bashing and blaming the ref or ump for a bad call is reduced, it will increase the enjoyment level of everyone in the surrounding areas. People also tend to forget the bad calls that go in their favor. It is small things like this that can have a huge impact on the overall enjoyment of the game and youth sport experience.

Don't Ever Allow it to Become Personal

Coaches should not coach with a grudge. Leave it off the field of play. Bringing in personal feelings about the other team, the other coach, a parent, or others will only lead to mismanaging your players. Mismanagement can lead to exhaustion, injury, and missing the little things that can lead to bigger issues and problems down the road. Let your team's play speak for itself.

So many times coaches bring personal feelings and history into a game that should be left off the field. They will tell their team, "We don't like this team! Their coach is a jerk. He thinks he knows it all."

I know of a situation where a team was going against one of their assistant coaches from the previous season. The head coach felt slighted, and thought the assistant coach took some of his best players with him to start the other team. He wanted to stick it to his ex-assistant. Game day arrived and it was a very hot day. The head coach pitched his best pitcher, and left him in too long because he was totally focused on beating his ex-assistant coach. That pitcher had to leave the game and be treated for heat exhaustion. As a parent, I wouldn't be able to trust that coach with the health and welfare of my son.

The true purpose of the game and enjoyment can be lost when a coach brings in personal history and feelings. Leave it off the field, worry about your own team, and their health and development.

Find a Trusted Friend for Support

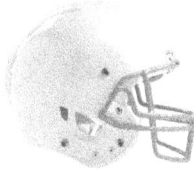

Coaches, you should find someone who you trust who isn't associated with your team so you can talk with them and vent your emotions. We know you get bombarded frequently concerning issues from parents, umps, players, and others about your decisions. It is hard to always listen and fight the urge to snap back like they are questioning your decisions.

A trusted person can help you talk through things and blow off some steam. Some people will always second guess your calls, no matter your explanation, but staying even tempered will go a long way. You don't know who else is watching. This is one area that is very hard for volunteer coaches, and often the reason others won't step up to volunteer. We understand. Take a step back and have that trusted person so they can help talk you through the situation.

Tony Dungy once wrote about all of the interview requests and suggestions he received from fans when he was coaching the Tampa Bay Buccaneers and Indianapolis Colts. People would write suggestions, or send in plays that

should work. He had to have the team screen his communi-
cations. It doesn't matter what level you coach, people will
always have suggestions or input.

It is a lot easier to watch at a distance, and then provide input without stepping up to volunteer. Understand
that point, and find your trusted person who can help you
decompress. Some suggestions might be valid while others
aren't, but having a chance to take it all in and discuss it will
help prevent you from burning out.

Working with Parents as a Team

In order for parents to best facilitate learning and growth of athletes, they should support and restate the coach and team goals when leaving the field or court. If they are not sure, or don't agree with the coach, they should set up a meeting as soon as possible. The child will look to them for guidance. It is hard to facilitate growth if they are receiving conflicting messages. This is why it is imperative for the coach to develop the proper relationship with parents.

The child will look to them on the car ride home or away from practice, and ask what they think of the coach and practice. The worst thing for a parent to say is that the coach doesn't know what they are talking about, or this drill or that drill is worthless. These statements can crush a season, team, and/or player. Credibility of the coach will drop in the mind of that young athlete. When they are on the bench or sitting around with their team, be assured that the parent's words will be repeated, and the doubt will be spread within the team. Very few kids will push back and say, "Maybe your parent doesn't know what they are talking about."

Now with doubt set in the mind of terammates, focus and hustle will start to diminish from the practices. The kids will think, "Why should we work hard if this coach doesn't know what they are doing?" Kids will start to horse around more, which will lead to the coach being harder and disciplining the team. The discipline will start to take away from the drills and fundamentals the coach is trying to teach. Team progress will be hindered; individual progress will be hindered.

The coach should make sure each parent is onboard with the approach for the season. The parents have equal responsibility to check and understand with the coach, but few parents will be proactive enough to meet with the coach about team goals. Therefore, it is up to you to take the initiative.

Know your team

The key to reaching kids is to be interested in their interests. All you have to do is ask, then remember it, and bring it up at another time. This will earn you an enormous amount of trust with that player. They will be more willing to take in any instruction, or provide open and honest responses in the future.

As a coach, getting to know your athletes is vital to the growth and development of each kid. Each one is different in their likes, motivation, and reason for being on the team. Taking the time to figure out and remember something about each of your players could have a tremendous impact on their life. It could be the first time that any adult had any interest in one of their interests outside of sports. Most kids are *talked to* and not *talked with*. Things to discuss might include video games, favorite subject, favorite food, or vacation location. The list could go on and on, but it just takes one of those things to make a connection.

Try to think and name one thing about each player on your team outside of sports. Throughout the season bring it up, and reference it, watch what happens in their expression and interaction with you.

Remain Open to New Ideas and Methods

Coaches, here is a myth buster for you. Most people teach what they were taught years ago or *back in the day*. Presenting something new or a different way to do things isn't a sign of incompetence, but it is actually the opposite. It shows that you have a grasp of the concept, and are actually looking to achieve a specific outcome for that particular audience. People learn differently, recall differently, process information and stimuli differently. Don't let the *way it has always been done* stop you from trying something new or a different approach.

Art Briles, head coach of the University of Baylor football team, said years ago the best athletes were put on defense. Now the best athletes are put on offense to learn the plays and wide open schemes. Having the top athletes on offense has created teams that have wide open scoring and video game stats. He has been very successful with this adjustment, even if this transformation pushed him beyond his comfort level.

The point is that the games and approach continue to evolve. You, as a coach, need to be open to the change, or the game will pass you by. Push your comfort level to understand new methods and approaches. Learn and study the strengths and weaknesses of the approach. Any work or studying you put in will benefit your players tenfold.

Focus on Teaching, Not Pleasing Parents

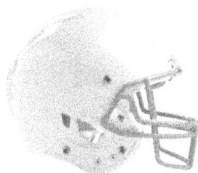

Not everyone is going to agree with the coach's methods and approach. They may even file a complaint. Remember to not be quarrelsome and argumentative, but stay resilient in your approach to teach. Do not alienate the athlete to spite the parents. Stay focused on teaching, and let them watch and see the results. You can't force them to see and understand, that is on them and their personal convictions.

There will always be different philosophies on how to teach and coach each game. This also applies to drills during practice, just as long as the focus is on correct movement for a specific outcome. People will want to have their input; many times they repeat what they learned and think it is the only way to approach a situation. They might not grasp the change, and change scares some people.

One example is teaching bunting with 9 and 10 year olds. Most kids at the 9 year old level don't like to commit to the bunt since they are still getting comfortable with their own swing. The stance used in the pros with rotating the hips and getting the bat at an angle and using the top hand as the fulcrum, doesn't work too well for the kids at the younger age. So an alternate technique is to have the batter square both feet off facing the pitcher. This gets the batter into a commit stage more than the previous technique. The batter's focus is now on making contact rather than committing and then making contact. It cuts a step out of the decision making process for the batter and makes the game a little easier.

Conventional wisdom will claim to not teach a technique that will need to be fixed at a higher age. Kids should be learning the techniques used at the higher levels. It is a valid point. The counter to that is teaching a smaller piece of the fundamental of getting the young athlete comfortable with making contact on a bunt. Once they get a little older it is easier to move them back and show the other method, but now they are comfortable making contact in a bunt situation.

Parents and other coaches will approach you about your methods, but just as long as you have an understanding and can explain it to them, you will be fine.

Building Life Skills

You should celebrate and recognize little wins over adversity. Let your kids know that they can't celebrate success without a total victory over adversity. An example could be when a kid gets hit in the helmet from a pitch and won't stay in the box. He keeps getting up to bat and jumping out every pitch. Keep putting them in, and when they finally get that hit, their sense of achievement will last a lifetime.

This goes back to teaching and learning life lessons. Building a little confidence in sports can start to spill over into other aspects of life. They could be struggling in school, making friends, trying to play an instrument, or some other new skill. Recognizing an obstacle and addressing it will help to build life skills to take on problems and overcome them. The reason sports are a great way to teach this lesson is because usually the obstacle is a physical object. They will need to conquer their fear of something they can see and touch. As they get older, most things they have to overcome will be things they can't see or feel. These can be things like fear of rejection or abandonment, insecurities, self-induced pressure, and knowledge recall.

Recognizing, acknowledging, and, overcoming are all steps you can help them with during the season. Help build those life skills and celebrate those little wins!

Character is More Important than Results

Actions and character are much more important than results. People don't remember you for how many wins and losses you have; they remember how you played the game. Since coaching is about so much more than teaching a game, it makes sense that the positive implications should exceed the box score and stats.

These come to light in moments of stress and difficulty. The kids will be looking to their mentor for guidance and encouragement. Sometimes they will take it upon themselves to respond, and you, as the coach, need to be there to correct the behavior and actions to ensure it is in line with proper guidance and behavior.

There was an incident where a 13u baseball team in West Virginia beat their rival in tournament play, and posed underneath the scoreboard flipping off the camera. The coaches were right there with the team giving the same signal. No matter what the other team did or didn't do, the coaches didn't intervene, but were guilty participants. The town they represented was very upset, and suspended the kids and coaches from going any further in the state tournament.

Teach kids to be responsible and of high moral character, and that will do more for them in their life than a moment of bad judgment and poor sportsmanship. This will come back to you tenfold. I can't recall hearing any stories or experiences about a kid coming back to his coach and thanking him for taking a shortcut or teaching them poor sportsmanship.

Participating for the Right Reason

Coaches, how can you expect your players to get better or perform better if they don't enjoy the sport? Being properly motivated and having input are key driving components for increased enjoyment that will lead to improved performance.

I met with a 17 year old who has been playing hockey his whole life, and his parents had spent over one hundred thousand dollars on his equipment, travel, special coaches, extra ice time, and league fees. They continued to spend money trying to help improve his game, and get him into a good college with an excellent hockey program. Everyone had recommendations on how he could get better, even to altering his training and diet. Specialized coaches claimed they could help him and give him the extra edge he needed to standout if he would just follow their methods and instruction. He spent most of his time at the rink playing hockey and most of his friends were hockey players. At the end of the day, he shared with me that he didn't enjoy playing anymore, and he didn't know how to tell his parents and friends. He was afraid they would be disappointed and/or angry with him. Our talk ended with letting him know that his parents and friends don't want to see him miserable or unhappy. They might miss watching him play, but in the long run they would want him to pursue something he enjoys and loves.

As coaches we can push our athletes too hard trying to make them better because we assume they are there because they love the sport and want to get better. Take the time to ask them. A good tip is to find a way to get them involved or have input in the direction of the team. If they feel they have a say or some control, their enjoyment will skyrocket. Being a key contributor or influencer can turnaround their perception of the current situation.

Know How to Correct Mistakes

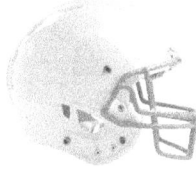

When providing direct instruction to a young athlete, use a good, bad, good method. The reason is that when you start off on a good note they don't tune you out immediately, their mind goes to what they were doing right, and it helps with proper memory recall. Next, address the negative issue, and the proper way they should perform that movement or skill. Finish with a positive note for the same reason as starting. Recall and muscle memory work the same way if it is a correct movement or an incorrect movement. Have the young athlete dwell on the correct movement in a positive way. You don't want them thinking about the incorrect movement or technique, since the likelihood is that they will perform on what their muscle memory will recall.

Too many times at any sporting event you can hear parents and coaches yell about the play the athlete just missed. The kid knows that he just missed the play, he doesn't need an obvious reminder. He will start to dwell on the missed play, and the next time he is in the same position, he will miss the play again. They need to understand the adjustment they need to make so talk them through it, and instill confidence in them. Also, consider carving out practice time to help that athlete make the adjustment and work on the improvement. Chances are that other members of the team will need to spend time on the skill as well.

Establish a Discipline Policy

Any good coach will have a fair and balanced discipline policy for the athletes on their team. Having a fair policy that is clearly communicated and enforced will build respect from the players and parents. The policy should be age appropriate.

Here are the steps:

- Develop an age appropriate policy, (i.e. 6 year olds shouldn't be running miles)
- Share with team and parents, and give them the opportunity for feedback
- Ensure policy is carried out in an unbiased manner
- Do a one-on-one with the parent of the disciplined athlete so they understand and remain on the same page as the coach
- Do a one-on-one with the athlete so they understand why they are being punished and can correct their behavior

Most people are afraid to enact a discipline policy out of fear of retribution from the parents or a stigma from society. If the policy is well-known, laid out, age appropriate, and communicated in the appropriate manner, it will be valuable for the growth of the team and athletes. It can be difficult at the time, but it will reap bountiful benefits in the future.

An important aspect of being an athlete, and successful in life is discipline. They will need to learn to operate within a specific set of parameters, and failure to do so will result in a set reprimand. A discipline policy isn't just for the problem kids, or the kids who want to stick with sports. A framed policy will benefit all kids as they go through life, and they will thank you later in life, probably not in the moment.

One example is a military drill sergeant. They are in your face, and have you doing things that you view as ridiculous. They push you farther than you believe you can physically go, but at the end of basic training you view them as friends and mentors. They want the best for you, and they use a method to get you to see and believe more in yourself and capabilities. Granted this is an extreme example of discipline, and I'm not advocating you develop a reputation of being like a drill sergeant, but it helps to get the point across.

Be Aware of the Potential Impact of a Coach

Coaches, what if your biggest impact or greatest achievement wasn't about the number of games won or D1 athletes coached, but saving just one kid from a life of crime or even suicide? Our impact as coaches stretches further than we know.

Start to ask other coaches, athletes, or adults the impact of a coach they remember from their youth. Be prepared to be blown away. Our impact as coaches will also have a lifelong effect.[1]

---

1   Read a great story about the importance of youth coaches to a professional athlete. http://www.theplayerstribune.com/demary-ius-thomas-mom-broncos/

Teach Your Team How to Lose

Don't worry about protecting your kids from losing, encourage them to not give up and quit. A greater opportunity to learn and grow is at the hands of a defeat. Why would anyone try to stop a life character growth moment?

You Lost.....What Now?

You lost.....what now, what does it mean? The choice is yours on how to respond in that important moment of time. Everyone claims that the tough times are what made them into the person they are today. So why would people be afraid of losing? Your goal isn't to lose, and you put in so much hard work and effort toward your goal, and yes, losing can come with a short-term of mixed feelings such as despair, failure, anger, and frustration, but in the long term losing doesn't define you as a loser or failure.

Some people don't know how to handle a brief, yet character defining moment. Think about it, out of your whole lifetime, loss is nothing but a moment, just a sliver of time in your life. How you choose to respond will affect and show your character as well as how others perceive you. What will it do for you: Inspire, Drive, Destroy, Motivate, Hinder, or Encourage? People you don't even know might find strength and motivation from your hardships in their own life, teammates could form stronger bonds of trust in times of need, or it can be the other side of the coin because you chose to throw a fit or tantrum, and blame everyone else. You shouldn't strive to lose, but embrace the opportunity to grow and learn in that moment.

The truth is that no one is exempt from a loss. There have been some huge perceived gaffs that have led to some major losses in the world of sports, but it is just a brief moment in time. Think about this year's **Super Bowl** *with Seattle at the 1 yard line with the championship on the line and throwing an interception and sealing a victory for New England, or at this year's* **Women's World Cup** *with England's best defender putting in the game winning goal into her own net with less than a minute to play and clinching the game for Japan. You could come up with example after example, and these would just be from well-known events. This doesn't include anything that happens at the youth level. Losses don't discriminate. You aren't the first to experience a loss, and you won't be the last.*

So what is a loss? We define a loss as coming up short in a moment of time while in pursuit of something of perceived value. No one is exempt from a loss, and at the same point, everyone in the world isn't considered a loser. If no one is exempt from a loss, and not everyone is a loser, than what does a loss do if it doesn't make us a loser?

A loss provides an opportunity to show your character. Think about the image of metal being heated to show its impurities and then being formed into its purpose. Trials and hardships provide this opportunity to show our character as well as help shape us into our purpose, assuming we are strong enough to stand up to the heat. Metal that isn't strong enough will be discarded and used for a lesser purpose, or it will require more refinement.

Now since a loss can be a hardship it provides us the opportunity to show that we can handle the situation, and the true nature of our character. If you handle a loss and hardship in a respectful manner, you will build internal strength to push you through future hardships. Additionally, others will see you as an inspiration, trustworthy, and as a pillar of integrity. On the other hand if you handle a loss in a less than a respectful manner such as; assigning blame to others, looking for excuses, throwing a temper tantrum, or even quit and walk out, then you will be relegated to a lesser role, and viewed as untrustworthy in the perception of others.

This can be very troublesome if you are still pursuing sports. Success in team sports is dependent upon the bond you have with your teammates and coaches. If they don't trust you then you won't play or be called on in crucial situations. Many people will point to their hardships as life defining moments, and come to be thankful for opportunities to turn them into the person that they are today. See a loss for what it is, an opportunity to grow and learn.

Now you might ask if a loss can truly be a good thing, then why do parents try as hard as they can to protect their kids from a loss. There are two main reasons that can be derived from a parent's desire and effort to avoid losing for their child. The first one is character exposure, and the second is pain avoidance, which is misinterpreted as protection.

In a child's life, a parent is the main influence on their character development as well as the child's moral and ethical beliefs. If a loss exposes character in a person, then for a child it will expose the parent's influence on the child. A parent will feel that their inadequacies as a parent are on full display. People will go to great lengths to hide their perceived inadequacies. We say perceived because whether inadequacies really exist or not isn't the important part, but if the parent believes one exists that is the important part. People will drive their behavior off of perception.

The second misconception on the parents' part is that they believe they are protecting their child through pain avoidance. Pain avoidance isn't the same as protection, and all it does is build a false sense of confidence, and delay the inevitability of a future loss. A false sense of confidence leads to a feeling of entitlement, which still sets their child up for failure in life.

Another truth in life is that nothing is given, it has to be earned. A child that feels entitled grows into an adult that feels entitled, and when they learn that truth then the reality will hit a lot harder than if they would have experienced a loss earlier in life. So pain avoidance isn't the same as protection, and actually causes more pain and hardship down the road.

These inadequacies and insecurities are internally perceived, and might not be an actual reality, but since they are perceived by *the parent then they are a reality to the parent. These insecurities are a vital component for the spending behavior that has created a billion dollar plus industry. Parents will spend money on the best equipment, trainer, select team, or any gadget in hopes that all of these will prevent their child from losing.*

Yes, teams and employers are going to want winners or someone that preservers. A winner is someone that has experienced losses and setbacks but grew stronger from them. Losses can make winners. A team or employer isn't going to want someone that has never lost, because you can't trust a person who has never lost because their behavior and reaction is a mystery. Since losses are inevitable in life at some point, then you don't know how a person that hasn't yet experienced a loss will react when a setback happens. Will they be destructive and become a cancer to their team, tearing everything down and making things weaker because they aren't internally strong enough to handle a setback? It is a high risk to bring someone in with such a big question mark hanging over their head.

This is a question that will come up, and they will want to know about a loss and how you handled the situation. Discussing how you were able to bounce back and use the loss as a launching point will put you in a better light with your audience. Think about Aaron Rodgers dropping in the NFL draft with the cameras right in his face watching his reaction every time another name was announced. He sat there putting on the best face possible on the outside as I'm sure it was painful to take on the inside. He has used that experience as a launching point for his career, and teams probably regret not taking him when they had the chance. So a loss or hardship can provide the opportunity to propel you to exhibit a winning attitude.

A loss shouldn't be scary or seen in a negative light, but as an opportunity to display our internal strength and courage. Protecting kids from a loss only serves to ease a parent's concerns, but ends up being more harmful in the long run of life. Teams and employers want people of high character. Winning alone doesn't make you a winner just as losing doesn't make you a loser. Hardships and losing are inevitable in life so how you handle it is what shows your character and what people remember about you. You lost.........now what........?

Learn from Success

Don't solely focus on the areas that haven't improved, but rather focus on the progress made in other areas, and continue to build off that progress.

Too many times, coaches focus on a lack of progression of a certain drill or movement, and they don't see the growth and development of other skills.

Try to understand why that skill developed, and see if you can build off of it, or use it to help in other areas. Maybe it developed because it is highly relatable to an in-game movement, or broken down into smaller steps, etc.

This doesn't mean to abandon the skill you are trying to teach, but evaluate what you are trying to teach and how. You can still work that skill, but don't obsess about it for the sake of other areas that can be improved.

Coaches need to stay receptive to how athletes are learning. If we can find the best way to connect with each athlete we will help grow and develop them faster.

Keep Parents From Undermining Your Coaching

Coaches should have in place a team rule to prevent the parents interacting with the athletes while they are on the bench or dugout, except for bringing water or a potential injury. This isn't for a power trip, but to keep a clear distinction for the young athletes. This will help keep their focus on their teammates, game/practice, and the coach. It will allow for your message as a coach to sink in, or give them some time to process the information. Having a designated boundary with a timeframe will allow them to easily shed any outside issues, and give them a place of solace.

Parents want to help by coming up and offering advice, insight, tips, etc. While normally this isn't a way to undermine your coaching, it frequently has that effect. So, try to minimize distractions to help better facilitate instruction and development. The young athlete will try to judge the information coming from their parent and the coach. Sometimes the information will contradict what the coach is telling the athlete, and this can cause major issues between the player, coach, and parent.

Mike Matheny talks about this in his *Matheny Manifesto*. He has a strict policy that if kids play on his team, parents won't interact or speak with the kids while they are under his supervision. The parent's intentions might be in the right spot, but this will reduce any chance of conflicting messages and instruction.

Understand Why Players Do What they Do

Try to understand the difference between a misplay and a sport/situational decision. Kids might make a play because they processed the game information and made a decision differently than what you saw as a coach. Instead of getting on them for a perceived mistake, first ask why they made the decision and the play they did. They might surprise you with their answer, and show that they have a deeper understanding of the game and situation than you gave them credit for, or they might not understand the situation at all. Determine how and why they are processing the information, and then respond.

This situation will play out thousands of times across the country in different venues. For example, in a close game with a runner on first base, there was a line drive hit to left field that was an *in-betweener*. The left fielder pulled up to field the ball on a bounce and throw the runner out at second since the runner hesitated. The coach got on the left fielder and benched him for a lack of hustle. When the assistant coach talked to the player, the player said he didn't think he could get to the ball, even with a dive. He didn't want the ball to get behind him and then have the runner score. The assistant coach was stunned by the response.

Think about the problem caused if the assistant coach didn't speak with the player. The head coach viewed the player as being lazy and not into the game. If that perception would have endured, the player would have been relegated to the bench, and probably the bottom of the order. The player would have been upset and confused, not knowing what he did wrong, because his instincts and knowledge of the game told him that he made a correct play.

This is a significant trait of excellent coaches as they are able to relate to young athletes.

The Value of Repitition

There is no substitute for repetition. No piece of equipment, no dollar amount can ever replace the physical repetition of performing a task or movement.

Coaches, you don't need to provide feedback after every rep. Do the rep in a block of 20. Let your athletes adjust, and then discuss after that block. Go back and do another block of about 20 reps.

Repetition will help with muscle memory as well as letting the player feel the movement. This will allow them to make adjustments if they start to feel and understand when an incorrect movement takes place.

Over-coaching can be just as harmful for proper development as improper coaching.

Allow Kids to Fall in Love with the Game

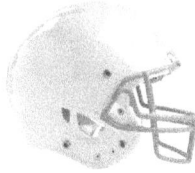

You can't force a kid to love a game; you can only introduce them to the game and strategies for succeeding both mentally and physically. They will fall in love with the game on their terms not yours. They may even discover that they don't love the game, and that is ok.

Kids love to play and can find enjoyment in just about any activity. Turning it into work or a job before high school will only push them away. Do you like to be forced to do something? What is your initial reaction? Most of the time it is resentment. It is the same with kids.

Think for a moment on how the X games started. The majority of the sports evolved out of free play. Kids were not under pressure by their parents because their parents never competed in the activities they were doing since they didn't exist. Also think about all of the fads such as *Planking*, or dance moves. They evolved from free play that individuals grew to love out of fun and enjoyment. The more stress and pressure that is put into an activity, the more likely it will lead to a higher dropout rate.

The counter argument is that the dropout rate is fine because it is natural selection to weed out the individuals who are too weak to make it anyway. This argument is usually made by parents who are just interested in their child moving to the next level. The problem with the argument is a limited scope of view.

Players that naturally fall in love with the game will end up being the best leaders on the team. Getting peer motivation from a team leader will make your job as a coach so much easier as you communicate your message and develop the team.

Listening, One of Your Most Effective Tools

Listening is a valuable but under utilized skill. This will help to change a coach from talking at his team, and help him talk to his team.

People spend so much of their time waiting to speak rather than listening to what the other person has to say, process the information, and then respond. It has been said that *we should be quick to listen, slow to speak, and slow to get angry*. Information is readily available to coaches if they will take the time to really understand the information.

Kids, and adults for that matter, will gravitate toward people who truly listen to them, and take time to understand their perspective on the situation and world. Kids will do radical things just to get attention or find someone who will stop and listen to them. They are growing and trying to understand how to get around in the world.

Try asking your players to tell you a story, any story. Remember the story and at a following game or practice ask for more details about the story. Watch how the players start to gravitate toward you as their coach.

Choose Your Words Carefully

Coaches should stop using words such as *can't*, *never*, and *won't*. They place a negative limitation in the young athlete's mind. It makes teaching more difficult, because you are asking them to push their limits and go further then they believe possible, then you add another negative boundary with these terms.

Instead of "you will never hit that shot like that," try "you will hit that shot more often like this." (Insert any drill or sport)

Expect your athletes to push past their limits, grow, and develop, but keep adding small unnecessary road blocks. It is a small change, but a highly impactful one.

There are many people in life who will be glad to tell you that you can't do something, or that something is impossible. Don't be that person for your players. Instead, be part of the minority that believes they can excel far beyond their imagination.

The Value of Being a Positive Influence

As coaches, we understand athletes must go through hardship as they grow and develop. It is important they are also surrounded by positive influences to help give them a correct vision, meaning, and understanding of the hardship. As a coach, we must be one of those positive influences. This can come from our actions and our mentorship. You could be that one positive influence in their life that makes the change for the good.

There hasn't been one incident where an athlete has ever come back and thanked their coach for teaching them how to cheat or take a shortcut. It might give them a short-term win, but in the long-term they will look back on that situation and understand that the shortcut wasn't in their best interest. Their respect and admiration for that coach will be destroyed.

In life, you can always learn something from everyone. It might be the way to do something, or the way not to do something. Being a coach that leaves the impression of the wrong way to do something isn't a positive influence that a young athlete needs from a mentor or coach.

Build Team Unity by Including Everyone

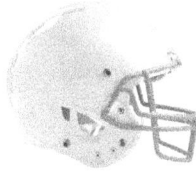

Coaches, to help build team cohesion, each member of the team must feel they have some input or say in the direction and function of the team. They want a sense of ownership of their team, not just being on your team.

Figure out creative ways to get their input. Some use team goals, but try to be more specific than just win the championship or go undefeated. Maybe ask what they think the team needs to work on, lead warmups, etc.

The more you can include each member the stronger the team bond.

Turning a Setback into a Step Forward

A setback shouldn't be viewed as a step back, but rather as a loading stage to propel you forward. Every situation shapes us and our future stature. The decision lies internally on how the situation will shape you moving forward. Everyone can make excuses; the world is filled with people who have excuses. Teach your kids to find results. Work harder, ask them to come up with a drill or situation to use during practice. Having them understand the situation and think about how to work on it, will be a great growth opportunity for them.

There are many examples of this, and every athlete has their own story of their setbacks. The one that sticks out in my mind is the story of Bethany Hamilton. She is a surfer and was attacked by a Tiger Shark that resulted in the loss of her left arm. Losing an arm is traumatic, but that coupled with the potential of never again being able to surf, something she loved, was almost too much to bear.

Her determination to learn how to surf with one arm started out as something for just her. She didn't start out to inspire millions through her will, determination, and faith, but that is exactly what happened. She dealt with a life altering setback, and turned the tables to take a thousand steps forward. People pull strength through her inspiration. It is like the old adage, the person who thinks they can't do something and the person that thinks they can are both usually right.

Understand the Value of Continuing Education

Be wary of the coach who believes additional coach's training is a waste of time or beneath them. These coaches tend to be very vocal and let the board know it is a waste of their time. This has a paralyzing effect on the progression and development of the league, and the kids that they are supposed to be coaching. A coach should be there to teach, listen, learn, and adjust. It is impossible to do if they think they already know everything.

Include Fun in the Regimen

Coaches you should have a couple of practices throughout the season that encourage free creative play. Some coaches have one at the end of the season with the kids vs. parents using various games.

The purpose is that it will be a fun exercise that will increase their enjoyment of the game outside of a strict practice regimen. It accelerates team bonding, and if you have one early enough, you can use it as a reward later in the season because they will keep talking about it. Make it simple, be creative, allow the kids to act like their hero with the game on the line. We can all remember how we pretended to be the hero in Game 7, or the Super Bowl, etc.

It ends up being one of the more memorable moments of a season. You can get a lot of valuable development and fun out of these practices just as long as they are utilized correctly. Make it fun so they will continue to be interested to learn more.

How to Instill Motivation

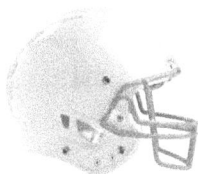

Ask any athlete who their greatest influence has been in their life, and they will say that it is a person that first BELIEVED in them. There isn't a magical drill to build their confidence, but just try a simple yet sincere "Johnny/Jane, I believe in you, you got this."

I believe in you…" a simple statement that will resonate with them for life.

This is something that will build them up as an athlete as well as a balanced individual. Motivation is different for different types of people, and the majority of the time it is external.

If a young athlete doesn't have enough self-confidence built up, having an external source of confidence will help to motivate them. The external source will be from the desire to not let his coach and team down since that is the group that believes in the young athlete.

Pay Attention to Weather Conditions

Understand the weather conditions and have a plan of action during practices. Granted, the league will stop games under dangerous conditions, but it falls on the coaches to make that decision for practices.

Some teams practice at different fields or courts from the league, so there isn't an oversight except for the coach. Understand heat and proper hydration. Don't risk it with lightening or pending storms.

Try to setup a backup indoor facility in advance if the weather looks like it could get bad. When in doubt, don't push the situation. Most times it will be the correct call, and sometimes it won't, but it is better to err on the safe side than endanger your team trying to squeeze in one more rep or drill.

Behavior Reminder

Just because a coach should know something or know how to behave doesn't mean they do. It needs to be addressed every season with every coach.

Coaches, this goes for you and your assistant coaches. Lay out expectations early, and ensure they are understood. It feels weird to tell another coach not to swear and cuss at the team or even grab a player, but that conversation needs to take place.

This is one of the first questions that will come up for any investigation, whether it is a civil or criminal inquiry. They will ask "Were the team rules and expectations laid out?" Answering that acceptable behavior is common sense won't be a fully acceptable answer.

It is a small task, but it is important.

Communicate a Code of Conduct with Parents

All parents that yell aren't bad people. They might not know how to behave or be aware of proper etiquette. It is important to cover a code of conduct with the parents at the beginning of the season, and possibly a refresher during the season if they aren't adhering to proper behavior. This will also lead to higher credibility as a coach, because you are following what you stated at the beginning of the season.

We had some parents, actually wives of the coaches, who would yell during the games, and talk trash like they were at a professional game. They would make fun of the last names of the kids, thinking they were just having a good time. The coaches didn't want to say anything because they had to go home to their wives and they played it off as it was no big deal, they are just having fun. The other parents had to stand up and say something, without it turning into a physical confrontation. It was great to see, because that is a situation that could turn ugly, or people could have continued to turn a blind eye to it, but they didn't.

I don't believe they are bad people, but I do believe they truly didn't know better. In that situation, it would have been better for the coaches to handle the situation but the end result was positive.

Focus on Teaching Foundational Skills

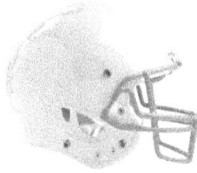

Coaches, you need to have trust and openness with your assistant coaches about their kids on your team. You can't have one set of rules for the team, but a second set for the other coaches and their kids. Understand the perception of Daddy/Mommy ball.

There is a tendency to overlook the basics as common knowledge for new fads, methods, fancy drills, or gimmick plays. Some of these new methods could be productive or effective, but overlooking core foundation skills will cause everything to crumble down the road.

When the spread offense was introduced and teams started putting up video game stats, other teams were trying to quickly adapt. However, a team would not be able to make the changes effectively if the lineman did not know how to properly block, or receivers know how to properly cut and get correct body position. College teams could make this transition a lot sooner than youth teams. Young teams might get carried away in trying to score six touchdowns, or produce inflated stats. Young athletes still need to know and practice the basics to build a strong foundation. A weak foundation won't support adding additional skills properly. People get overconfident in their knowledge of basic principles, and get frustrated when they fail in crunch time.

Some coaches of select clubs try to implement gimmicks as a way to point to their *perceived* advancement over the competition or other clubs. We see it all the time during games as they will pull out trick plays, and they work at that level. The issue is that as kids develop and grow older, the gimmick plays quit working. The kids that focused and worked on the basics end up being more advanced because that is what colleges and scouts look for, not the gimmick plays that look cool and work from time to time.

To really make an impact on the development of a young athlete you will need a focus on the core basics and principles that will allow for solid foundation to build additional skills over time.

Coaching Standards

Not enforcing standards is the same as not having standards. How can your league serve the community without minimum standards of coaching and behavior?

Protect Athletes from Themselves

Coaches, you have to protect your athletes from themselves. They will be overly competitive, and try to push themselves beyond their limits. You need to be able to understand their limits and protect them regardless of the score or importance of the game.

The example that comes to mind here is R.A. Dickey when he was pitching in college. He was an ace that had some amazing pitches. He was pitching in the championship game and didn't want to come out. His coach kept deferring to his pitcher, but R.A. was caught up in the moment. He threw almost 200 pitches in that game, and possibly tore one of the ligaments in his elbow so bad that it wasn't found during his medical examination by the Texas Rangers. His signing bonus and major league career were in severe jeopardy. He had to learn a new method of pitching, and spent many years in the minors learning how to pitch again.

Athletes are highly competitive for various reasons. They are driven, they don't want to let their coach, team, family, or friends down. They are confident in their abilities, and don't know their limitations. Take the decision out of their hands and make the call to protect them.

Understand Before You Punish

Kids act up and act out for a reason. Talk to them before you rush to judgment and handout punishment. Some might defy you just to be cool in front of the other kids, but some might be looking for attention and not able to cope with a high stress life situation.

We had an athlete on our baseball team one season who frequently got into my sunflower seeds and sport drink. I kept yelling at him and making him run for doing this stuff without asking permission. It was as if it was a game to him, to see how much he take or drink before I noticed. He didn't mind being punished, and I was really frustrated that I couldn't get through to him. I tried to teach the need to have respect for other people's things.

I had to take a step back and look at the situation to figure out why I had been so ineffective in reaching him. I learned that he came from a single parent home, and his mom was working two jobs to provide for the family. He didn't have any brothers or a strong male figure in his life.

It was his way of getting attention and having someone set limits for him in a strong male figure role.

He wasn't being a little punk because he was a difficult kid, he was just acting that way because he was looking for attention and interaction from a male authority figure. I ended up buying extra seeds and sports drinks so we both would have enough. I did debate about adding some hot sauce to the seeds to see if I could get him back while he was sneaking the seeds.

At the end of the day, the important thing was being there for him and understanding him and his situation. We were able to work on the respect issue after understanding more about him and his environment.

How to Handle Difficult Kids

Dealing with talented kids that act out can be a difficult situation. Kids develop at different rates and ages. You will have some on your team who are physically more advanced than other kids at the same age. A good number of these kids will hear from their parents about how great they are, and things will come easy and naturally.

The problem is that it doesn't instill a work ethic, and you start to see the entitlement behavior develop. They can end up being a distraction to the team. Some coaches deal with it, because of the kid's talent level, but that doesn't help anyone in the long run. As a coach we must teach that playing is a privilege instead of a right.

We had a coach come to us for help with this situation. He had a kid on the team who was a complete distraction for the rest of the team. His parents just laughed at his behavior, and encouraged the disruption. He told us that this kid would go up to bat and swing backwards on purpose because he thought it was funny. Sometimes he would actually hit the ball and that would be the worst possible outcome because he would try it again his next time up.

The coaches spoke with the parents, but got nowhere with that approach, and it got to a point where they were hoping he wouldn't show up to practice or game day. They wanted help because they knew hoping a kid wouldn't show up isn't the way to reach him. We recommended batting him last, and if he went up there and swung backwards to immediately call time and ask the ump to just take the out. Even if he hit the ball, but did it as a joke, just count the out and have him sit down. This will show him, the team, the parents, and everyone else that his behavior won't be tolerated. Respect from the other players and their parents on the team will skyrocket by enforcing proper behavior standards. We also recommended to let him bat the second time up and see if he changed his approach and attitude.

Sometimes you will have to take an extra step to reach these kids as a lesson for everyone involved. Playing is a privilege and not a right no matter how talented and gifted a young player might be.

It's OK to Be Human

Coaches, you will make mistakes during the course of the season. There are no perfect coaches! An exceptional coach is able to own up to their errors and address them with the player, parent, team, coaches, and/or referee. The kids will respect a coach who can admit their mistakes and own up to them. It makes them more human and relatable. Kids are constantly being told how and why they messed up whether it is about school, chores, or sports. Having a coach admit to an error only strengthens the bond between athlete and coach.

This brings to mind a story I heard from a coaching friend. He was coaching one of his wrestlers in the wrestling state finals tournament. His wrestler had a great shot to win the whole tournament. During the quarterfinals, his wrestler was set to wrestle a kid that he had beaten four times during the course of the season. His wrestler was up by four points with under thirty seconds remaining.

The other wrestler was tired, body exhausted, and mentally about ready to accept defeat. My friend instructed his wrestler to continue on the attack even though he didn't need any more points. His wrestler advanced to put an exclamation point on the match only to have the other wrestler through a last ditch desperation move. My friend's wrestler got hit with a five point move, and lost the match as time expired.

He was so distraught, he said it felt like a punch in the stomach that left him grasping for air. He felt he failed his wrestler, and the opportunity to compete for that state title. He apologized to his wrestler face to face with tears in his eyes. His wrestler told him, "Don't worry coach, I shouldn't have been so sloppy to let him hit me with that junk."

Many years after that incident happened, they got together and were telling old stories. The wrestler thanked his coach and mentor for caring so much about his wrestling work. He said having someone who cared so much about his effort and well-being taught him more about life and how to approach it and treat others than just winning that title would have taught him.

No one is perfect, your athletes or you, and that is ok.

One Step at a Time

Coaches if you have someone struggling with their game or in life, set them up with small tasks and goals to accomplish. Have them practice blocking everything else out and just focus on the small task at hand. Overcoming one task at a time will start to build back self-confidence while also strengthening their ability to block out all negative environmental influences.

You can't get through the day without getting through the next minute or hour. You can't get through the next game without getting through the next play or pitch first.

Conclusion

We hope you found this set of tips helpful. Understanding the environment, background, and learning style of your athletes will help with their Total Athlete Development (TAD). A kind word or small understanding of what they are experiencing can radically change a young person trying to maneuver in a crazy and confusing world. These tips are designed to help you and them establish that connection, and provide a positive and meaningful interaction.

This book is just one piece of the material and resources we use to help coaches. Another is the online courses and material at www.naccc.info. *The National Athletic Coaching Certification Center* is specifically designed to help coaches every season with our course material and additional resources to be a positive impact for the kids they coach. Our core focus is to provide Positive and Meaningful Adult Interactions (PMAI) for the kids with a focus on the Total Athlete Development (TAD). The coach can be a leader and an example for the parents to follow, and we want to help make that example a positive one. The kids deserve it!

www.ingramcontent.com/pod-product-compliance
Lightning Source LLC
LaVergne TN
LVHW021521080426
835509LV00018B/2599